START PLAYING
CHESS
TODAY!

A QUICK AND EASY GUIDE TO PLAYING CHESS

ROSALYN B. KATZ

CARDOZA PUBLISHING

Dedicated to Zaria, Asher and Ella Katz

Production and Design: Steven Marshall Katz
Many thanks to: Alan Stern, Charles Joseph Pole, Sheila Lund-Pearson, Dawn Ippolito, Steve Ferrero, Peter Tamburro, Olga Tsybeskova, Doreen Szymczak, Robert Casagrande, and Troy Farrow for their help and support.

Originally published as *Chess for Children;* later, *Start Playing Chess*
Copyright © 1993, 1996, 2011 by Rosalyn B. Katz
– All Rights Reserved –

Library of Congress Catalog No: 2011933307
ISBN: 10: 1-58042-286-1
ISBN: 13 978-1-58042-286-4

Cardoza Publishing is the foremost gaming publisher in the world with a library of more than 200 up-to-date and easy-to-read books and strategies. These authoritative works are written by the top experts in their fields and with more than 10,000,000 books in print, represent the most popular gaming books anywhere.

Visit our website or write us for a full list of our books, software and advanced strategies.

CARDOZA PUBLISHING
P.O. Box 98115, Las Vegas, NV 89193
Phone (800)577-WINS
email: cardozabooks@aol.com
www.cardozabooks.com

TABLE OF CONTENTS

FOREWORD

When I was asked to write the foreword for this book, I was more than honored. Roz Katz has been a longtime friend and a great supporter of chess for all ages. Her tireless work and encouraging spirit has motivated over 3500 NJ chess players to lobby the legislature on behalf of chess. Thanks to Roz, New Jersey officially recognizes the benefits of chess and has included it in the state curriculum.

I know of no one better suited to promote and teach chess than Roz. She has been a constant source of support for me personally and professionally and aside from her many accolades, can explain the nuances of beginning chess better than most. I have no doubt that by reading this book; you will catch the "chess bug" from Roz and incorporate it into your life too.

Happy reading!
Dean Ippolito

IM Dean Ippolito is the current NJ State Champion and the real "Dean" of the Dean of Chess Academies. A renowned author and teacher, his dignity and calm combined with his skill, make him a chess treasure.

INTRODUCTION

Welcome to the world of chess. This book was written for you, so that you can learn chess quickly. You will also learn how to record your moves, that is, write them down. Hints about getting better – where to go, and what to do are also found in these pages.

From earliest times, chess has been played by people who love to think, plan and win. Play a fighting war game without spilling real blood. Join the ranks of those who love the game of chess, such as: Will Smith, Sting, Russell Crowe, and Arnold Schwarzenegger. Even Benjamin Franklin and Napoleon loved this game.

I know a soccer player who said chess helped her play soccer. Thinking skills and planning can make your life better in many ways. Whether you're six or ninety-six, this game can only add dimension to your life.

Any place in the world, no matter what language is spoken, you will find a player. No matter how good you are at this game, a beginner or a Grandmaster, all you need to do is set up a board with your pieces then wait. Someone will sit down, shake your hand and start to play. Just try it, you'll love it.

I. THE GAME

Brain power is the key to winning a game of chess.

THINK + PLAN = WIN

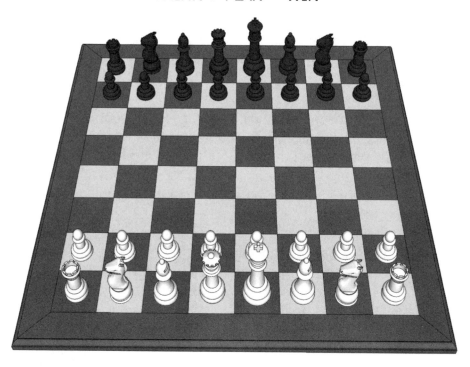

To play, you need a board and pieces.

There are two players, known as "White" and "Black."

Each wants to capture the other's king. Checkmate the enemy's king. Mate it, so it can't escape.

Just like a real war.

Important things to know

Each piece starts on its home square.

The player with the white pieces gets to move first. Each turn, you move once.

Once the game starts, pieces move to different squares.

Capture is when you bump an enemy piece off the board. You move your piece to the square that held the enemy piece – taking its place.

Check is when a king is attacked.

Checkmate is when a king cannot escape to safety.

Done. Finished. **The end of the game.**

Check

You are in check when your king is attacked by an enemy piece. You must get out of check right away.

Ways to get out of check:

- ♕ Block by moving another piece in the way
- ♕ Capture the enemy attacking piece
- ♔ Move the king to a safe square

Checkmate

When the king is in check and has no way to escape, the game is over. This is "checkmate" or "mate."

Stalemate or Draw

This means that nobody wins. The game is stuck.
It's a draw.

A stalemate happens when there are no legal moves on the board for the person whose turn it is to move, and no king is in check.

It's also a draw if:

- ♚ The same position is repeated three times during the game (you both keep making the same moves).

- ♚ 50 moves are made by each side without a capture or pawn move,

- ♚ There are not enough pieces to mate, or

- ♚ BOTH PLAYERS AGREE TO A DRAW!!!

Resignation

When a player has a horrible position, with no way to win or draw – that player may resign. That means the game is over. Never resign too soon. You never know what can happen.

Sometimes players agree to a draw – and go play tennis.....

or start another game.

Results

A chess game starts when White makes the first move, and ends when:

♔ White wins   1 - 0

♚ Black wins   0 – 1

♔ There is a draw   ½ - ½

II. THE BOARD

The board is the world of the chess pieces.

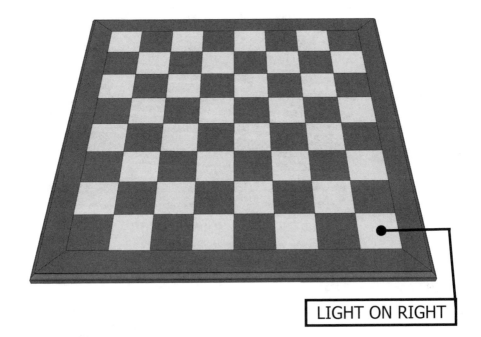

LIGHT ON RIGHT

There are 8 squares across and 8 squares up and down. All together there are 64 squares. You can count them to make sure.

The chess board has light and dark squares. A light square is always in the bottom right corner. When you see boards set up with a dark square in the right bottom corner, you know that is wrong. You can tell someone the board is set up wrong, and fix it.

Each square on the board has its own name
with a letter and a number.

The numbers go
up the side.

The letters go across the bottom.

To find e7, go right to e and up to 7.
See the "X" on e7?

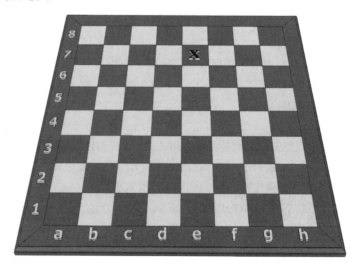

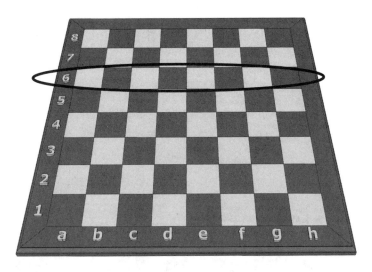

Each row on the chessboard is called a rank. The row numbered 6 is called the 6th rank.

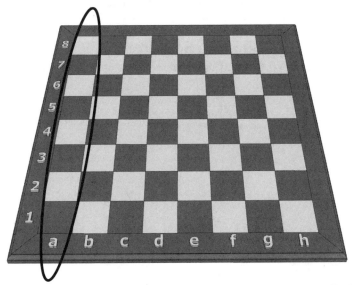

Each column of a chess board is called a file. The "a" file is the one all the way to the left on the board.

Point to square e4.

Did you find e4? See the "x" on the board below.

If you found e4, go on to Section III to learn about the pieces. If you did not find e4, go back and read about the board again.

III. THE PIECES

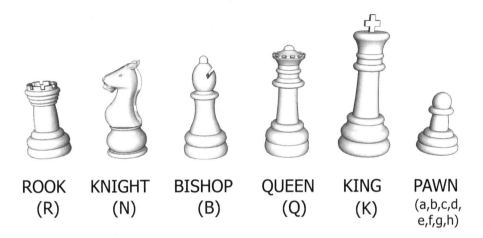

ROOK	KNIGHT	BISHOP	QUEEN	KING	PAWN
(R)	(N)	(B)	(Q)	(K)	(a,b,c,d, e,f,g,h)

The pawn is known by the letter of its file. A small "c" stands for the **c**-pawn.

From now on when you see one of the letters, you will know which piece it is.

Each piece has a different job and moves differently.

You are the boss of all your pieces. Like a general in the army, a conductor with an orchestra, or a coach managing a team.

The **K** ♔ is not shown in the chart below, because without the **K** there is no game. It is over. The **K** is really you.

Some pieces are stronger than others. The chart below shows the usual value of the pieces.

PIECE	SYMBOL	VALUE IN PAWNS
Q	♛	9
R	♜	5
B	♝	3
N	♞	3
p	♟	1

The Knight - N

The knights start on b1 and g1 for White,

and b8 and g8 for Black.

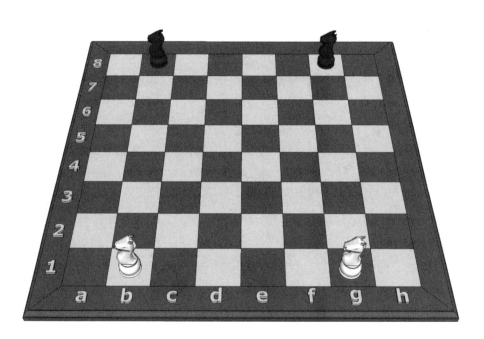

The N is the only piece that can jump over other pieces. It moves two squares in one direction and one square in another direction.

This **N** can go to a3, c3 or d2.

Look at all the dots in this diagram. They show all the squares that the **N** on d5 can move to.

An **N** in the middle of the board has eight possible moves. Wow!

Remember two and one, or one and two – like an "L" turned all different ways.

The **N** attacks any piece that is on a square it can move to. To capture an opponent's piece, the **N** replaces that piece. The captured piece is taken off the board.

Can you show each square that this **N** can move?

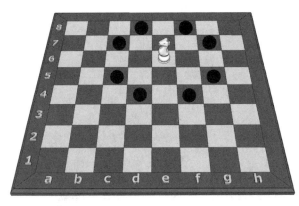

Did you find all the squares where this **N** could move? You should have listed: c5, c7, d8, f8, g7, g5, f4 and d4. If you got all eight correct, that's great.

Remember that the **N** is the only piece that can jump over other pieces.

In this diagram, can you name all the squares where the black **N** on e7 can capture a piece? Write down the names of the pieces and the squares that they occupy.

The **N** on e7 can capture the **R** on c8 or the **B** on g6. Did you notice that a capture of the **B** goes with a check? It's important to remember that the best knights are the ones you put near the middle of the board.

The Rook – R

The rooks start on a1 and h1 for White,

and a8 and h8 for Black.

The R moves in a straight line, left and right along the rank, up and down the file that it's on. It stops anywhere along that line, or when it captures an enemy piece in its path. It replaces the enemy piece that it captures, and takes over that square.

The **R** at a1 can move to any of the squares shown, in a straight line.

Or like this.

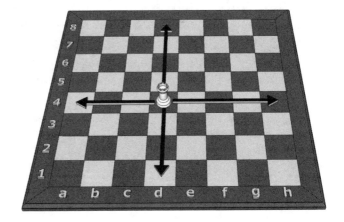

In this diagram, if it's Black to move, which pieces can be captured by the **R**?

The **R** on d5 can capture: the **Q** at c5, the pawn at d6, the **N** at g5, or the **B** at d1.

Which pieces can be captured by the white **R** on e4?

If you said, the **N** at a4, the **N** at h4, or the **B** at e6, you are correct. Good for you.

With Black to move, which squares have pieces that can be captured by **R** at d5?

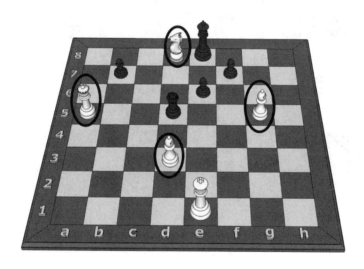

Did you say a5, g5, d8, and d3? If you found all those squares, you are ready to go on to the **B**.

The Bishop - B

The bishops start on c1 and f1 for White,

and c8 and f8 for Black.

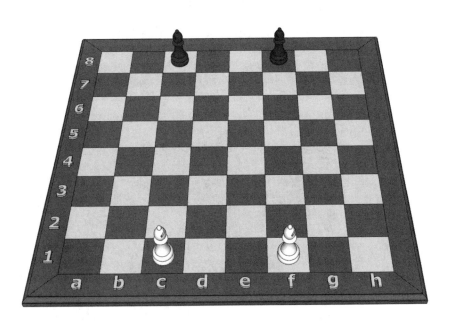

The B moves diagonally. It cannot move straight: up, down, or sideways, only diagonally. Each B stays on the color square that it starts on for the entire game.

Look at all the squares the **B** at c1 can travel to. From a3 to h6, and all the dark squares along the way.

Look at the diagram on the right. Can you see all the squares that are controlled by the **B** at d5? Remember, it always stays on the same color and can never jump over other pieces.

Do you see the **B** on e5? Point to every square it controls.

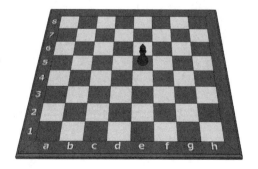

Look at all those dark squares. Did you get all of them?

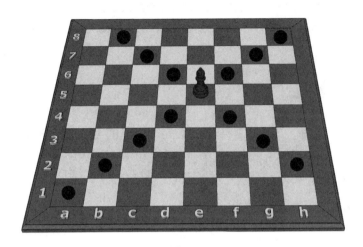

The **B** attacks any piece in its path. Which pieces in the diagram at the right, are attacked by the White **B** at e4?

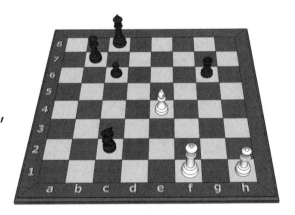

Look at the next page for the correct answer.

If you named the pieces: **c6**, **R** and **N**, that's very good. If you answered, the pieces on c2, c6, and g6, you got it!!!! Both ways of answering are fine, as long as you understand the moves.

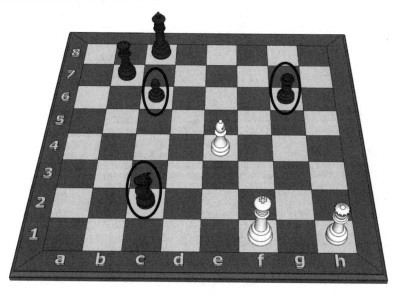

Remember: the pawn at c6 is known as **c6**.

Only the **N** can jump over pieces.

Bs always stay on the same color – for the entire game.

The **B** replaces the piece that it captures.

White to move. Which pieces can be captured by the **B**?

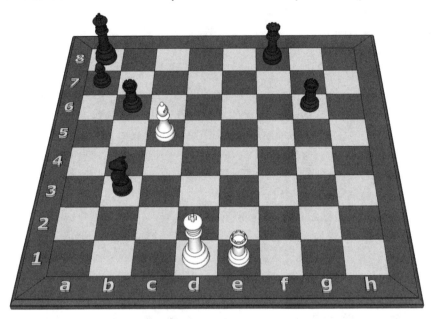

If you answered: The **Q** on f8 and the **R** at b6, then you understand how the **B** moves and captures.

You are ready to go on to the **Q** moves.

The Queen - Q

The queens start on d1 for White,

and d8 for Black. Each **Q** on its own color.

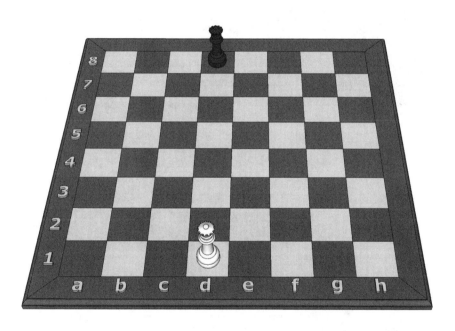

The Q is the strongest piece on the board. She can move like a B or a R. The Q attacks any piece directly in her path. She captures the same way that she moves.

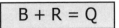

$$B + R = Q$$

Like this.

Or this.

In this strange diagram, the White **Q** is attacking every piece on the board. The **Q** attacks every piece in its path, as long as nothing is in the way. It captures by replacing the captured piece.

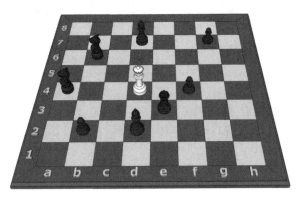

Can you figure out every square that this **Q** can move?

The dots show all the squares where the **Q** can land.

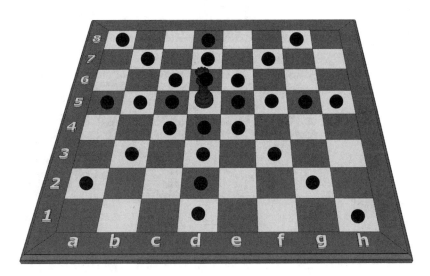

Which pieces are
in danger of being
captured by the **Q**?

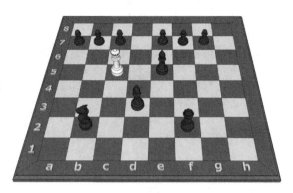

Did you find all the pieces that were in danger? Too bad,
you can capture only one piece at a time.

The X's have
replaced all
the pieces
that could be
captured by
the **Q**.

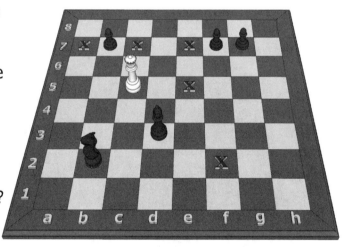

Have you
nailed the
job of the **Q**?
Isn't she a
remarkable
piece?

It's a good idea not to move your **Q** out too quickly at the
beginning of your game. You don't want to lose your **Q**
too early.

Make sure you understand the jobs of the **N**, **R**, **B** and **Q**,
before going on to the pawns.

The Pawn - p

The pawns run all the way across the second rank for White, and across the seventh rank for Black.

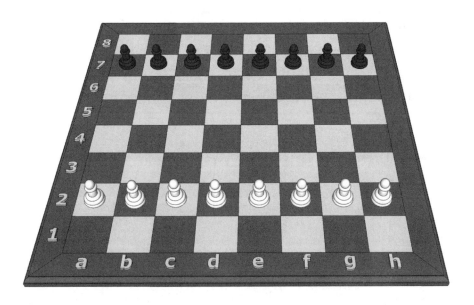

Pawns move only forward, never backward. The pawn moves straight ahead on it's file, one square at a time — EXCEPT on its first move or when it captures a piece.

The pawn is named for the file that it's on. This pawn is called "**e**." This **e**-pawn can either go one or two moves on its first move, to e3 or to e4.

After its first move, the pawn can only move one square at a time.

PAWNS DO REALLY STRANGE THINGS

♔ Move one or two squares forward on their first move.

♔ Turn into other pieces when getting all the way across the board.

♔ Move forward, but capture diagonally.

♔ Change their names after capturing a piece.

♔ Pretend the enemy pawn moved one square instead of two in the "en passant" move.

How can this **e**-pawn move?

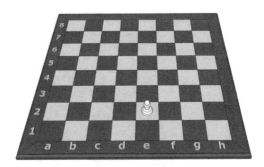

e can go to e3 or e4. Remember, after its first move, the pawn can move only one square at a time.

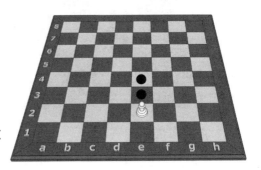

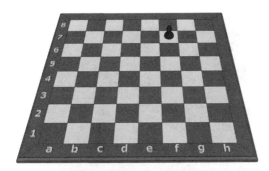

What about the Black **f**-pawn here?

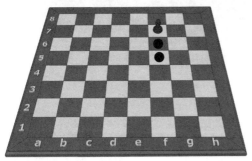

f can advance to f6 or f5.

Where can the **d**-pawn capture?

Capturing by a pawn is diagonal only. Like a mini-**B**, the pawn captures diagonally, forward, but only one square.

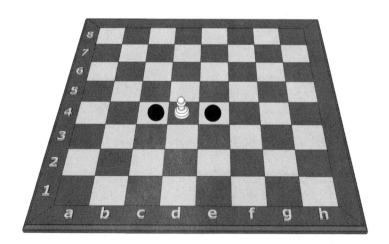

Which pieces can be captured by the **e**-pawn?

The **e**-pawn can only capture the **N** on f3.

In this diagram, if it's White to move, which pieces can be captured by which pawns? See if you can figure out what's going on here.

The **b**-pawn can capture the **B** at a3, or the **Q** at c3. The **f**-pawn can capture the **N** on g3, and **h** can also capture **N** at g3. The pieces which can be captured have circles around them.

It sounds complicated, but if you got it – that's cool.

Remember, a pawn cannot capture a piece that's right in front of it. Only diagonally, just up ahead.

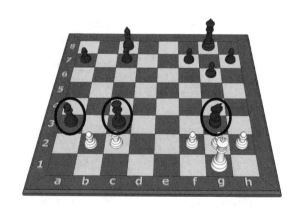

Queening

We still haven't finished with wacky pawn stuff.

When a pawn moves all the way to the end of its file, you can turn it into any other piece – except for a king. If you make another **Q**, it's called "queening." In this diagram, the **c**-pawn has become a queen. Usually, people get another **Q**, but sometimes you pick an **N** or some other piece.

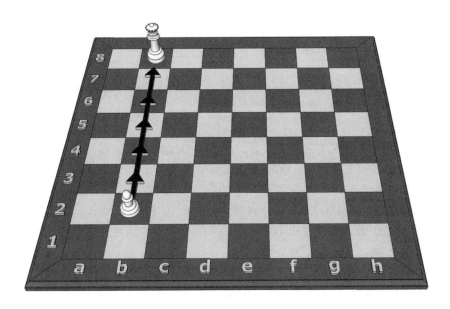

"En Passant" — "In Passing"

One more thing that happens only with pawns is capturing "en passant." This is French and means "in passing."

You hardly ever see this move; still, you need to know it. One pawn captures another, but ALL the bullets below, must be true:

- ♔ A pawn, on its first move advances two squares

- ♔ It lands next to an enemy pawn (so that they're side by side).

- ♔ The enemy can capture that pawn AS IF IT HAD MOVED ONLY one square.

- ♔ This must happen right away, the enemy's next move must be the capture. Otherwise, forget about it, it's too late.

Check out the "en passant" move in these diagrams.

If you capture "en passant," you are pretending that "**b**" only moved one square.

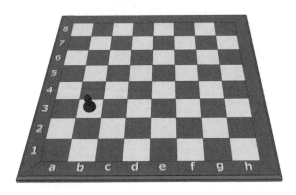

The King - K

The kings start on e1 for White,

and e8 for Black.

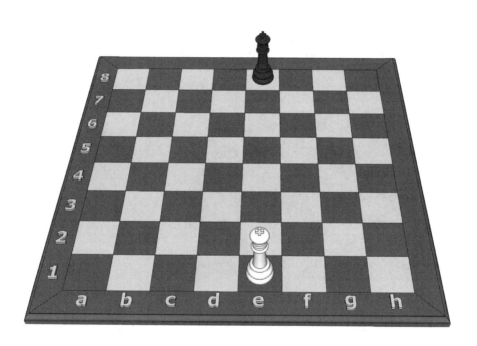

The K moves one square at a time – in any direction. The K is the most important piece in a chess game. You have to take really good care of your K, while you are attacking the enemy K.

As long as the **K** is not moving into check, it can move one square in any direction. The **K** replaces the piece that it is capturing, just like the other pieces.

Can you tell where the **K** at f4 can go?

This one is pretty easy, isn't it?

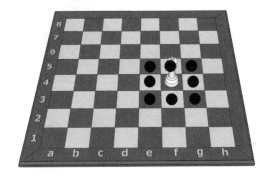

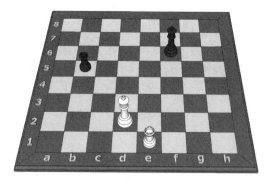

Where can the Black **K** move?

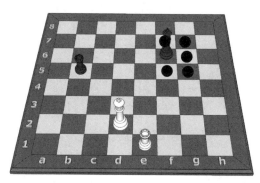

Did you find all the squares?

Did you notice the **R** on e1? The **K** cannot move into check.

What can the White **K** capture in the diagram on the right?

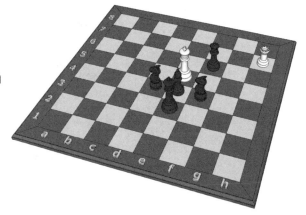

If you said only the Black **Q**, you got it!!!! The other pieces are all protected.

Castling

Castling is the only time two pieces move at once.

The **K** and the **R** both move. It is the only time a **K** moves more than one square, and the only time a **R** jumps over a **K**.

You can NOT castle if:

♔ Your **K** is in check.

♔ Your **K** or **R** has moved earlier in the game.

♔ Other pieces are in the way.

♔ Your **K** must pass through check during the move.

Castling is used in most games. It is usually a good way to protect your **K**.

When you castle, you move the **K**  and the **R** .

To castle kingside, move the **K** at e1 to g1, and then the **R** at h1 to f1.

Look at the picture below. It looks like this when your castling move is completed.

When castling queenside, this is how you do it. Move the **K** from e1 to c1.

And then the **R** on a1 to d1.

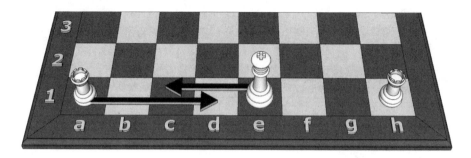

The completed move looks like this. See the queenside **R** is right next to the **K**.

In this position, show how you would castle kingside.
(A kingside castle is written: "0-0")

This is how your board looks after castling kingside.

Now show how you castle queenside.
(A queenside castle is written: "0-0-0")

This is how your board looks after castling queenside.

You're going to make this "castling" move a lot, so to it's very important to understand it.

In the next few diagrams, decide whether you can castle. Think it through.

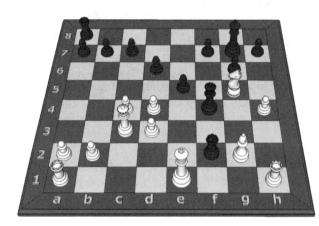

In the diagram on the left, it is White to move.

What do you think?

Even though the **R**s and the **K** have not yet moved, castling is not possible. The **K** would have to pass through or into check so that would not be a legal move. The answer is "no."

In this diagram, neither White nor Black can castle. It looks as if they both castled already. In any case, the kings have both moved off their original squares.

It is Black to move. What do you think about castling in this position?

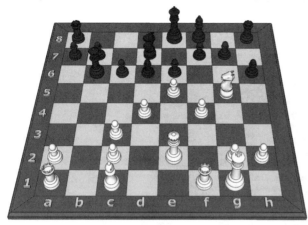

Black cannot castle kingside, because there's a **B** in the way. 0-0-0 castling queenside looks like a great idea.

This is what the board will look like after 0-0-0. Maybe this was not the best time to castle. Be careful about the **N** on g5.

It is White to move in the diagram below. Is castling okay here? Is it legal? Is it a good move?

What do you think?

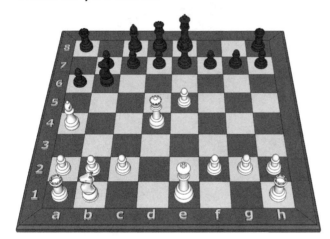

All the answers are "yes."

Here is the position after 0-0. Doesn't the **K** look cozy and protected?

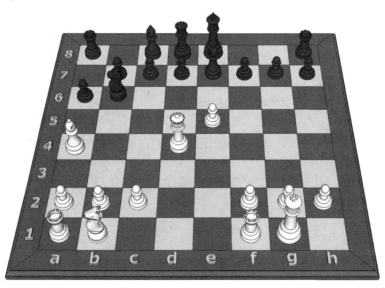

Now it's Black to move. What do you think of castling for Black?

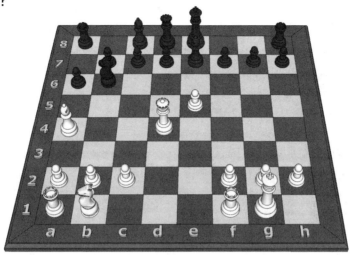

It looks fine, doesn't it? Black's **K** also looks cozy and protected.

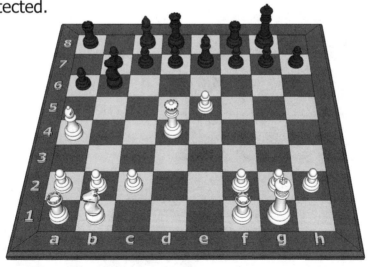

It's usually a good idea to castle early in the game, to protect your **K**. Many times, I have forgotten to castle, and then I go ouch! Too late, and then I'm in trouble.

IV. MATES AND ATTACKS

This section shows some simple positions for you to look at. Since you need to "mate" to win, these examples will help you find winning moves.

Use your board and pieces to work out these problems.

In these three diagrams, White can mate in one move. Can you find each of the moves? The answers will be on the next page.

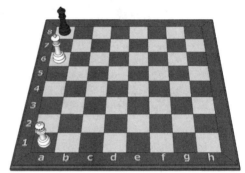

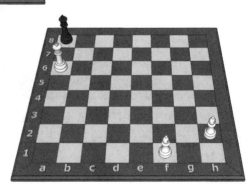

The arrows show how you can mate, in each of these three diagrams. Did you see all of these?

These are known as "back rank mates" and come up very often when you're playing a real game. You'll be glad you took the time to look at these carefully.

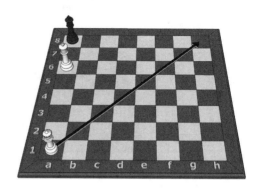

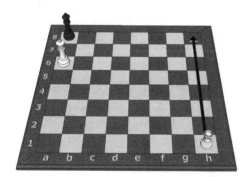

You can see how each piece had a special job to do, and how they worked with the **K** in these cases.

With White to move, the **B** at f1 moves to g2 and mates.

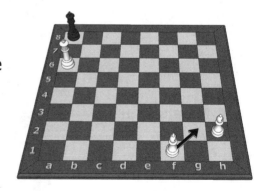

Look at this diagram again.

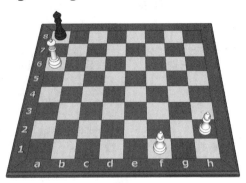

What if it is Black to move? Guess what? Black is stalemated. Black has no legal moves. That means it's a draw. Be really careful, if you are White, not to let this happen.

In the diagram to the right it is White to move. Can you see a mate?

Amazing and unusual, **N** to b6, mate. Did you find it?

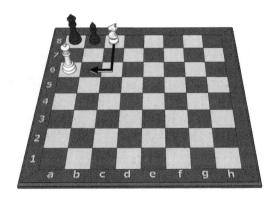

In this diagram, it is White to move. What is the best move for White?

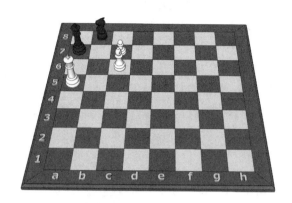

The pawn was promoted to a **N**. If you took the **N** with the pawn, Black's **K** takes your **Q**, and the game would end in a draw. When you promote to a **N** in this case, you have a "mate" that is much better for White.

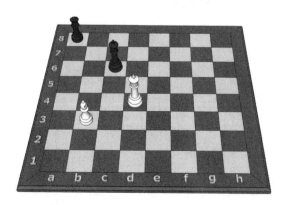

If White is to move, what is best?

All of a sudden, this whole game has changed. White's **B** "skewered" the **Q**. The **K** is in check, when it moves, the **Q** will be captured.

Oops!!!!
Black is no longer winning this game.
Now it's a draw. What a difference one move can make!

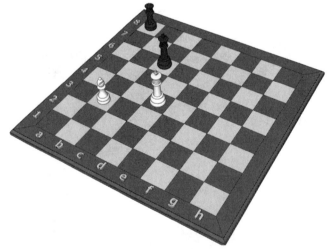

Do you see how different it would have been if it had been Black to move? What move would you make for Black?

Actually, White has many choices, but any other move would allow the **Q** to get out of danger. Black should have won this game with more careful play. Oh well, it was a good lesson, anyway.

Find the best moves for Black in the three diagrams on this page. Look at the next page after you've looked at all three positions on your chess board.

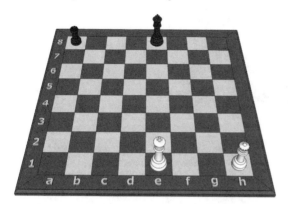

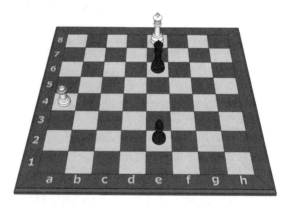

Are you having fun? I'll bet you got this one.

Did you see this sneaky **B** move?

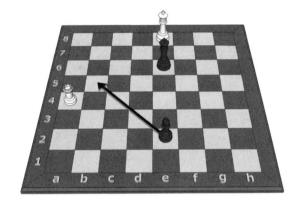

This last one is tricky. Did you see the **N** move for Black? If you fool around, moving the **R**, you will surely lose this game and be in trouble. The **N** move, called a "fork" is a sure win for Black.

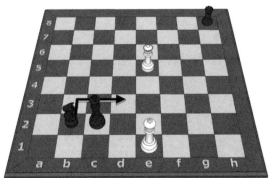

V. WRITING THE GAMES

This section will show you how to keep a record of your games. You can get a score book, score sheets, or just plain paper to write your moves. It's important to write your games, so that you can:

♛ Go over them
♛ Learn from your mistakes, or
♛ SHOW THEM OFF!

To write or read games, you need to know the letters and symbols in the charts below.

Letter	Meaning
K	King
Q	Queen
R	Rook
B	Bishop
N	Knight
a, b, c, d, e, f, g, h	Pawn

Sometimes you'll see these symbols.

Symbol	Meaning
X	Captures
+	Check
++	Checkmate
!	Good Move
!!	Great Move
?	Bad Move
??	Rotten Move
?!	May be Bad
!?	Interesting
0-0	Castles Kingside
0-0-0	Castles Queenside

Reading the Moves

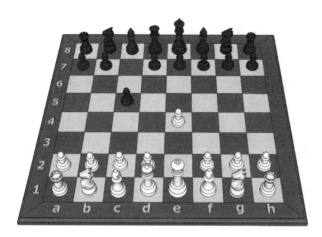

...c5

This means that Black moved the **c**-pawn to c5. The three dots mean that it was Black's move.

exf6

This means that White's **e**-pawn captured the piece that was on the f6 square. You may also see this move written as ef6.

0-0-0
This means White just castled queenside.

...Qf2++
The Black **Q** moved to f2, checkmating the white **K**.

Write the move down as shown by the arrow in the diagram below.

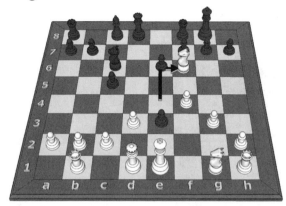

There was a Black **B** on f6 before this move was made.

Look at how the move is written to the right of the diagram below. Is that how you wrote the move?

Nxf6+

N captured the piece on f6 with check.

Did you notice the check?

How would you write this move?

Hint: Two Black pieces moved during this turn.

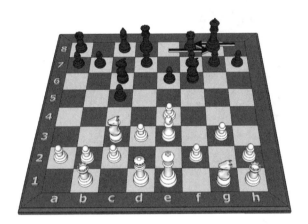

...0-0

Black castled kingside.

Just a little more practice before you go on to the next section. It is important to be able to read and write chess games. Write the move as shown by the arrow.

Take the time to think this out before looking at the answer.

Rb1

The **R** moved from a1 to b1.

How can you write this move?

...Bxf6

Black's **B** captured the piece that was on f6.

Once you get used to writing the moves, you'll be really glad that you can go over your games.

Are you ready to play a real game? Good luck and have fun.

VI. GETTING STARTED

Set up your board.

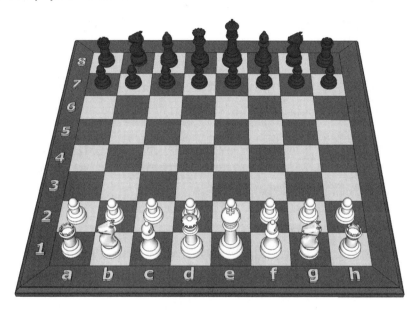

Remember:
- ♔ White always starts.
- ♔ Protect your **K**.
- ♔ Look for good moves that get your pieces attacking.

Which pieces can move on the first move?

If you said any pawn or **N**, you got that right. The other pieces need space, since they can't jump over anything.

Try to move the pawns in the center, or the **N**s first.

Practice by playing as many games as you can with anyone who will play with you. Getting used to moving the pieces is very important.

Don't be afraid of making moves – you're sure to lose PLENTY when you're starting out. Even after you play for a long time, you can lose PLENTY. I sure do.

VII. A REAL GAME

You can get good ideas when you look at other people's games. You can watch friends play, go over your own games, find games in newspapers, chess books or magazines.

I put one of my own games in here, so that you can practice reading algebraic notation while you go through a complete game. The best way to go over this game is to set up your board, and use your own pieces to follow the moves.

By going through the game move by move, you will learn how to:

  ♔ Develop your pieces
  ♔ Move your pieces during a game
  ♔ Capture pieces
  ♔ Trap enemy pieces and the opponent's king
  ♔ Mate

This game was played September 9, 1992, at the Morris County Chess Club. Bill Petersen was White and Roz Katz was Black.

	White	Black
1	**e4**	**c5**
2	Nc3	Nc6
3	g3	Nf6
4	Bg2	e6
5	d3	Be7
6	Be3	0-0
7	f4	d5
8	e5	d4!!
9	exf6	Bxf6
10	Ne4	dxe3
11	Nxf6+	Qxf6
12	Bxc6	bxc6
13	Rb1	e5
14	fxe5?	Qf2++

1. e4

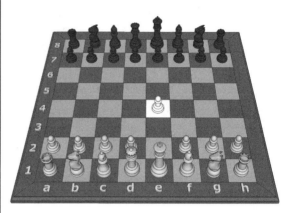

1. ...c5

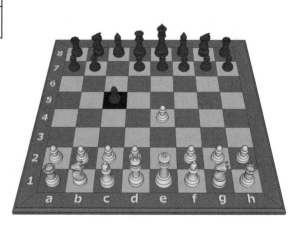

These are pretty ordinary moves in the opening. Getting a couple of pawns out and making room for your pieces.

	White	Black
1	e4	c5
2	**Nc3**	**Nc6**
3	g3	Nf6
4	Bg2	e6
5	d3	Be7
6	Be3	0-0
7	f4	d5
8	e5	d4!!
9	exf6	Bxf6
10	Ne4	dxe3
11	Nxf6+	Qxf6
12	Bxc6	bxc6
13	Rb1	e5
14	fxe5?	Qf2++

2.Nc3

2...Nc6

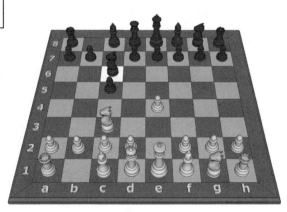

	White	Black
1	e4	c5
2	Nc3	Nc6
3	**g3**	**Nf6**
4	Bg2	e6
5	d3	Be7
6	Be3	0-0
7	f4	d5
8	e5	d4!!
9	exf6	Bxf6
10	Ne4	dxe3
11	Nxf6+	Qxf6
12	Bxc6	bxc6
13	Rb1	e5
14	fxe5?	Qf2++

3.g3

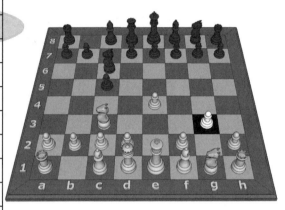

3...Nf6

	White	Black
1	e4	c5
2	Nc3	Nc6
3	g3	Nf6
4	**Bg2**	**e6**
5	d3	Be7
6	Be3	0-0
7	f4	d5
8	e5	d4!!
9	exf6	Bxf6
10	Ne4	dxe3
11	Nxf6+	Qxf6
12	Bxc6	bxc6
13	Rb1	e5
14	fxe5?	Qf2++

4.Bg2

4...e6

	White	Black
1	e4	c5
2	Nc3	Nc6
3	g3	Nf6
4	Bg2	e6
5	**d3**	**Be7**
6	Be3	0-0
7	f4	d5
8	e5	d4!!
9	exf6	Bxf6
10	Ne4	dxe3
11	Nxf6+	Qxf6
12	Bxc6	bxc6
13	Rb1	e5
14	fxe5?	Qf2++

5.d3

5...Be7

	White	Black
1	e4	c5
2	Nc3	Nc6
3	g3	Nf6
4	Bg2	e6
5	d3	Be7
6	**Be3**	**0-0**
7	f4	d5
8	e5	d4!!
9	exf6	Bxf6
10	Ne4	dxe3
11	Nxf6+	Qxf6
12	Bxc6	bxc6
13	Rb1	e5
14	fxe5?	Qf2++

6.Be3

6...0-0

	White	Black
1	e4	c5
2	Nc3	Nc6
3	g3	Nf6
4	Bg2	e6
5	d3	Be7
6	Be3	0-0
7	**f4**	**d5**
8	e5	d4!!
9	exf6	Bxf6
10	Ne4	dxe3
11	Nxf6+	Qxf6
12	Bxc6	bxc6
13	Rb1	e5
14	fxe5?	Qf2++

7.f4

7...d5

	White	Black
1	e4	c5
2	Nc3	Nc6
3	g3	Nf6
4	Bg2	e6
5	d3	Be7
6	Be3	0-0
7	f4	d5
8	**e5**	**d4!!**
9	exf6	Bxf6
10	Ne4	dxe3
11	Nxf6+	Qxf6
12	Bxc6	bxc6
13	Rb1	e5
14	fxe5?	Qf2++

8.e5

8...d4!!

	White	Black
1	e4	c5
2	Nc3	Nc6
3	g3	Nf6
4	Bg2	e6
5	d3	Be7
6	Be3	0-0
7	f4	d5
8	e5	d4!!
9	**exf6**	**Bxf6**
10	Ne4	dxe3
11	Nxf6+	Qxf6
12	Bxc6	bxc6
13	Rb1	e5
14	fxe5?	Qf2++

9.exf6

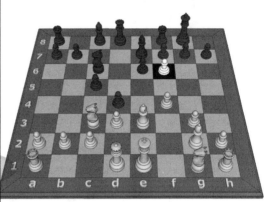

9...Bxf6

	White	Black
1	e4	c5
2	Nc3	Nc6
3	g3	Nf6
4	Bg2	e6
5	d3	Be7
6	Be3	0-0
7	f4	d5
8	e5	d4!!
9	exf6	Bxf6
10	**Ne4**	**dxe3**
11	Nxf6+	Qxf6
12	Bxc6	bxc6
13	Rb1	e5
14	fxe5?	Qf2++

10.Ne4

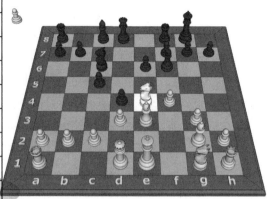

10...dxe3

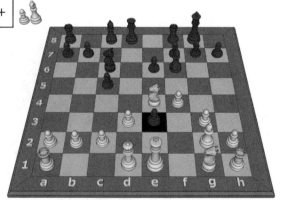

	White	Black
1	e4	c5
2	Nc3	Nc6
3	g3	Nf6
4	Bg2	e6
5	d3	Be7
6	Be3	0-0
7	f4	d5
8	e5	d4!!
9	exf6	Bxf6
10	Ne4	dxe3
11	**Nxf6+**	**Qxf6**
12	Bxc6	bxc6
13	Rb1	e5
14	fxe5?	Qf2++

11.Nxf6+

11...Qxf6

	White	Black
1	e4	c5
2	Nc3	Nc6
3	g3	Nf6
4	Bg2	e6
5	d3	Be7
6	Be3	0-0
7	f4	d5
8	e5	d4!!
9	exf6	Bxf6
10	Ne4	dxe3
11	Nxf6+	Qxf6
12	**Bxc6**	**bxc6**
13	Rb1	e5
14	fxe5?	Qf2++

12.Bxc6

12...bxc6

	White	Black
1	e4	c5
2	Nc3	Nc6
3	g3	Nf6
4	Bg2	e6
5	d3	Be7
6	Be3	0-0
7	f4	d5
8	e5	d4!!
9	exf6	Bxf6
10	Ne4	dxe3
11	Nxf6+	Qxf6
12	Bxc6	bxc6
13	**Rb1**	**e5**
14	fxe5?	Qf2++

13.Rb1

13...e5

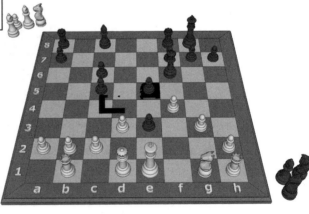

	White	Black
1	e4	c5
2	Nc3	Nc6
3	g3	Nf6
4	Bg2	e6
5	d3	Be7
6	Be3	0-0
7	f4	d5
8	e5	d4!!
9	exf6	Bxf6
10	Ne4	dxe3
11	Nxf6+	Qxf6
12	Bxc6	bxc6
13	Rb1	e5
14	fxe5?	Qf2++

14.fxe5?

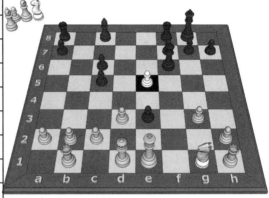

14...Qf2++

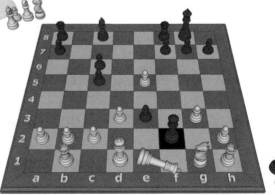

++ Means checkmate!! White's king had no legal moves and no way out of check. This was a really fun game for the winner. Even the loser seemed to have fun.

VIII. PLAYING TIPS

Get your pieces out fast.

Castle early to make your king safe.

Learn how to draw a game.

Move your king after most pieces are off the board. The king is strong in the endgame

Think about your move. Don't move too fast.

Guess the other player's move.

Write down your games for review later.

Get other players to look at your moves.

Join a chess club, or start one, or play on the internet.

Be brave. Don't be afraid to make a risky move.

Have fun!!!!!

IX. NEXT STEPS IN PLAYING CHESS

Chess players like you want to get better. Some players are really serious, and want to play in tournaments. Others want to beat their Moms, Dads and friends. You decide the best way for you to go.

Where	How	Contacts
Home	Keep board and pieces handy	Friends and family who play
School	Clubs, classes	Teachers, coaches
Tournaments	Announcements	Chess Life for Kids (magazine)
Online	United States Chess Federation (USCF)	www.uschess.org
Special Events	Watch newspapers and announcements	Local news, clubs, libraries, and coaches

There are an amazing number of free chess sites, where you can play on the internet. Some free sites are listed below.

www.games.yahoo.com/board-games
www.pogo.com/chess
www.playfin.com/chess
www.freeridegames.com
www.chessmaniac.com
www.gameknot.com
www. chessanytime.com
www.chesshere.com
www.chessrally.com
www.redhotpawn.com
www.chesskids.com
www.worldchesslinks.net
www.instantchess.com

Many schools have chess clubs. Some schools even have chess classes. If your school doesn't have a chess club, maybe a parent or teacher will help to sponsor one. Important resources are:

United States Chess Federation (USCF)

PO Box 3967, Crossville, TN 38557, Phone: 1-800-903-USCF (8723). www.uschess.org will give you lots of information and links to other sites.

The Chess Federation of Canada

356 Ontario Street, Suite 373, Stratford, ON N5A 7X6 Phone: 1-519-508-2362 Email: info@chess.ca. You can "google" your own state, and add the word "chess" to come up with local information. Local libraries and newspapers also have information on clubs and tournaments near you.

X. IMPORTANT TERMS

Advance   moves forward

Attack   threaten an enemy piece or position

Block   protect your piece by putting some thing in front of it

Capture   replace an enemy piece with your own – take theirs off the board

Castling   moving a **K** and **R** during one turn

Chess Club   a place where you can hang out, play or watch or talk about chess

Diagonally   move on an angle on the same color

Diagram   a picture of a chess board, with pieces

Enemy   your opponent

"En passant"   "in passing" a special pawn capture

File   the row that goes up and down on the chessboard (1 through 8)

Fork   when a piece attacks two or more pieces at a time – usually an **N** move

Grandmaster	the best chess players in the world
Kingside	the side of the board where the **K** starts playing
Occupy	when you're on a square, you own it (for a while, anyway)
Opponent	the player sitting across the board
Promoted	when a pawn reaches the final rank, as far as it can go, and becomes another piece
Queenside	the side of the board where the **Q** starts playing
Rank	the rows across the chessboard (a through h)
Resign	when a player sees the position is hopeless, and can't take any more – the player can give up (sometimes it's best to start a new game)
Resource	place or person you can go to for help or learning
Score Sheet	paper used to keep a record of the moves in a game

Simul   short for simultaneous play – when one player plays more than one opponent at the same time

Skewer   an attack forcing the enemy to move and the piece behind it is captured – ouch!

Stalemate   when the player whose turn it is has no legal moves, and is not in check – this is a type of a draw

Symbol   shortcut mark that stands for some thing (x = capture and + = check)

This is a picture of Roz with Mikhail Tal, former World Champion and Charles Pole.

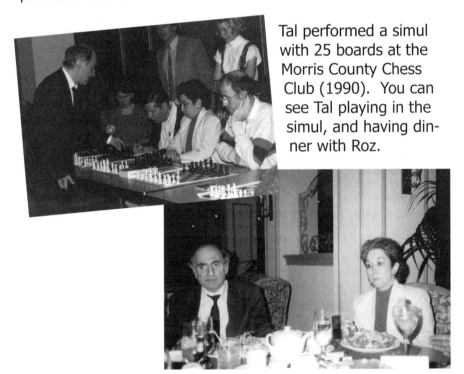

Tal performed a simul with 25 boards at the Morris County Chess Club (1990). You can see Tal playing in the simul, and having dinner with Roz.

GREAT CARDOZA CHESS BOOKS
ADD THESE TO YOUR LIBRARY · ORDER NOW!

303 TRICKY CHECKMATES by Fred Wilson & Bruce Alberston. Both a fascinating challenge and great training tool, these two, three and four move checkmates are great for beginning, intermediate and expert players. Mates are in order of difficulty, from simple to very complex positions. Learn the standard patterns for cornering the king, corridor and support mates, attraction and deflection sacrifices, pins and annihilation, the quiet move, and the dreaded zugzwang. Examples from old classics to the 1990's illustrate a wide range of ideas. 192 pgs. $12.95.

303 TRICKY CHESS TACTICS by Fred Wilson & Bruce Alberston. This is not just a challenging collection of two and three move tactical surprises for the advanced beginner, intermediate, and expert player—it's also a great training tool! Tactics are presented in order of difficulty so that players can advance from the simple to the complex positions. The examples, from actual games, illustrate a wide range of chess tactics from old classics right up to today. Great stuff! 192 pgs. $12.95.

ENCYCLOPEDIA OF CHESS WISDOM by Eric Schiller. The most important concepts, strategies, tactics, wisdom, and thinking that every chessplayer must know, plus the gold nuggets of knowledge behind every attack and defense, is collected together in one volume. From opening, middlegame, and endgame strategy, to psychological warfare and tournament tactics, the reader is taken through the thinking behind each essential concept. Through examples, discussions, and diagrams, you are shown the full impact on the game's direction. 432 pgs. $19.95

CHESS ENDGAME QUIZ by Larry Evans. This book features 200 challenges in the multiple choice format. These instructive, elegant and entertaining positions will not only challenge and entertain you but teach you how to improve your engame while trying to find the best move of the three choices presented. Sections include king and pawn endings, minor piece endings, queen endings, rook and pawn endings so you can concentrate on specific areas. What is the best move? Take the plunge and find out! 304 pgs. $14.95

THE 10 MOST COMMON CHESS MISTAKES...AND HOW TO FIX THEM by Larry Evans. A fascinating collection of more than 200 typical errors committed by the world's greatest players challenges readers to test their skills by choosing between two moves, the right one, or the one actually played. Readers will be amazed at how even world champions stumble by violating basic principles. From neglecting development, king safety, misjudging threats, premature attacks, to impulsiveness, snatching pawns, and basic inattention, readers get a complete course in exactly where they can go wrong and how to fix their game. 256 pgs. $14.95.

WINNING CHESS OPENINGS by Bill Robertie. Shows the concepts, moves and best opening moves from Black's and White's perspectives of more than 25 essential openings: King's Gambit, Center Game, Scotch Game, Giucco Piano, Vienna Game, Bishop's Opening, Ruy Lopez, French, Caro-Kann, Sicilian, Alekhine, Pirc, Modern, Queen's Gambit, Nimzo-Indian, Queen's Indian, Dutch, King's Indian, Benoni, English, Bird's, Reti's, and King's Indian Attack. Includes actual examples from 25 grandmasters and champions including Fischer, Kasparov and Spassky. 176 pgs. $9.95